Days of the Week

Sunday

by Mary Lindeen • illustrated by Javier González

Content Consultant: Susan Kesselring, M.A., Literacy Educator and Preschool Director

magic wagon

visit us at
www.abdopublishing.com

Printed in the United States.

Text by Mary Lindeen
Illustrations by Javier González
Edited by Patricia Stockland
Interior layout and design by Becky Daum
Cover design by Becky Daum

Library of Congress Cataloging-in-Publication Data

Lindeen, Mary.
  Sunday / Mary Lindeen ; illustrated by Javier A. González ; content consultant, Susan Kesselring.
     p. cm. —— (Days of the week)
  ISBN 978-1-60270-096-3
  I. Days——Juvenile literature. I. González, Javier A., 1974- ill. II. Kesselring, Susan. III. Title.
  GR930.L565 2008
  529'.1——dc22

                        2007034077

Seven days in a week

are always the same.

Which day is the first one?

Do you know its name?

JANUARY

SUNDAY	MONDAY	TUESDAY	WEDNESDAY	THURSDAY	FRIDAY	SATURDAY
	1	2	3	4	5	6
7	8	9	10	11	12	13
14	15	16	17	18	19	20
21	22	23	24	25	26	27
28	29	30	31			

Day one is called Sunday.

I knew that you knew it!

A new week is here,

so let's just get to it.

8

Have you ever thought
or did you wonder why,
we named a day in the week
for the sun in the sky?

Long ago, people thought
something beautiful and bright
would be the best way
to start the week out right.

So, they took the word "sun"

and they took the word "day"

and put them together

to make it "Sunday."

Sunday is a day

when you hear church bells ringing.

Many churches ring bells

for people praying and singing.

Sunday's also a day

to help others in need.

Make a meal, plant a tree,

or help a friend read.

On many Sundays,

we honor our family and friends.

We show respect to our nation

as the weekend ends.

Lots of people relax

and take a break when it's Sunday.

Then back to school and to work.

Tomorrow is Monday!

The Days of the Week

1 Sunday

2 Monday

3 Tuesday

7

Saturday

5

Thursday

6

Friday

4

Wednesday

SUNDAY ARTWORK

Make a bright, beautiful picture of the bright, beautiful sun. Use yellow and orange paint, yellow and orange crayons, yellow and orange markers, yellow and orange paper, yellow and orange glitter, yellow and orange buttons, or anything you can find to make your picture really shine!

A SUNNY SUNDAY SNACK

Have a grown-up slice an orange crosswise into round circles. Use a round cookie cutter to cut cheese slices into orange circles. What else could you eat that looks like the sun? Enjoy your Sunday snack on a sunny (or cloudy) Sunday afternoon.

WORDS TO KNOW

relax: to rest and become less tense.

tomorrow: the day after today.

weekend: the days at the beginning and end of the week; Saturday and Sunday.

year: a period of 365 days that is divided into 52 weeks or 12 months.